This book is presented to:

It was given to you by:

On this special day:

What Should I
Believe?
Is there really a God...

And does He care about me?

What Should I
Believe?

Is there really a God...

Phil A. Smouse

And does He care about me?

PROMISE
KIDS

AN IMPRINT OF
BARBOUR PUBLISHING

Published by Promise Press, an imprint of Barbour Publishing, Inc., P.O. Box 719, Uhrichsville, Ohio 44683, www.promisepress.com

ecpa Member of the
Evangelical Christian
Publishers Association

Printed in China.
5 4 3 2 1

For Bailey...

So she will know what to believe.

Grown-Ups!

"Which should I believe?"

Bailey's note took me completely by surprise:

> To Mr. Smouse, from Bailey Turba
> *Which should I believe?*

I had been praying (and praying!) for the right words to begin this special book. But I never dreamed they would be hand-delivered by a beautiful little second grader named Bailey.

Who am I? Where did I come from? Is there really a God? How can I get to heaven?

Kids don't ask those questions?

Don't believe that for a minute!

Every tiny heart on the face of this earth
is trying to find its way home to Jesus.

And God's eternal promise to our precious little
lambs is that *they will find Him* — when we take
time to lead them to His amazing Secret Place.

Thank you, Bailey, for your wonderful question.
Jesus is real. Jesus is alive. *Jesus loves you.*

You can believe in *Him*.

This page is for

Kids!

What should I believe?

> I'M NOT
> REALLY SURE

*Is God real? Who is Jesus
Christ? Is there really
a heaven? What about hell?*

Everyone seems to have
a different answer. And
everyone says that their
answer is the right one!

I want to know the truth. . .

But what should I believe?

That's a good question!
For God is either real or he's pretend. . .

I know God is real—and He's wonderful.
I'll bet you want to know Him, too.

So I'll do my best to help. But you must
decide for yourself. Who knows? Maybe
one day we will *both* say, *"I believe Jesus!"*

I CAN DO
THAT!

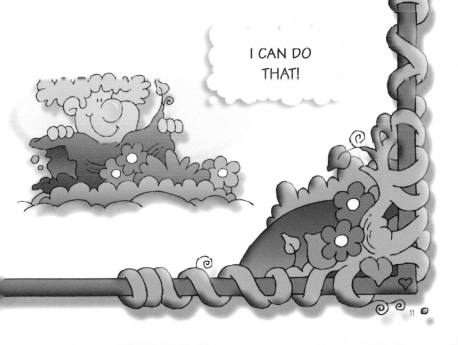

Is there only one real answer to this important question?

Or is it true that everyone is right in his or her own way?

Who is telling me the **TRUTH?**

Let's Find out!

What Should I Believe?

Come now, let us reason together.

Isaiah 1:18

I'M SO CONFUSED!

People love to talk. They say a lot of different things. They can't all be right. *Can they?* What should I believe?

That's **A GOOD QUESTION!**

Ánd there's a good answer. What is it? How can we find it?

The first step is easy. . .

And Here's the
First Step

We must want to know the truth! *"You will know the truth, and the truth will set you free."**

Free from what. . . ?

Free from the lie that God is not real!

*John 8:32

OKAY, I'M LISTENING. . .

If you've got ears
Listen to THIS!

What does "real" mean?

Is it true and not a dream, or pretend?

Then it is real!

15

WHAT IS THE TRUTH?

> *The truth will set you free.*
>
> *John 8:32*

I HAVE NO CLUE. . .

Is there really such a thing as *the truth?* Some people say no. They say the truth is whatever we want it to be. But this does not seem right.

16

Just **THINK ABOUT IT!**

We are alive. . .*and that is the truth!* So yes, there is such a thing as truth. And once we know the truth, we can believe it.

But where there is truth, there is also a lie!

Truth or Consequences?

GOD IS NOT REAL. . .
That is a lie!

NOBODY LOVES ME. . .
That is a lie!

THE TRUTH IS WHATEVER WE WANT IT TO BE. . .

That is the biggest lie of all!

> YOU CAN'T ARGUE WITH THAT!

And I **Quote. . .**

"I am the way and the truth and the life."

*Jesus Christ,
John 14:6*

WHaT is a Lie?

They exchanged the truth of God for a lie.

Romans 1:25

YOU'VE GOT TO BE KIDDING!

Have you ever told a lie? Sure! Everyone has. But why do you suppose we choose to lie? We lie to cover up something, of course. And what do we want to cover up? We want to cover up the TRUTH!

Why WOULD WE DO THAT?

Å lie will always stand in front of the truth. So when you see a lie, you know the truth is right behind it! How do you get to the truth? You simply take away the lie!

I WISH HE WAS!

Who Indeed!

If the truth has the power to set us free, who in the world would want to cover it up?

It was just an

ACCIDENT...

Remember this!

Lies can come in all shapes and sizes. So they're not always easy to see. But one thing is certain—they are never, ever, an accident!

WHERE DO LIES COME FROM?

The devil. . .is a liar and the father of lies.

John 8:44

I THINK I SEE ONE UNDER THIS ROCK!

Did you know lies have a father? Well, they do! Someone brought them into this world. And that same someone looks after them and makes sure they're healthy and growing. *For they are his children.* But who would want to be the father of lies?

Okay, **BaCK It UP a Bit!**

If a lie is made to cover up the truth, and the devil is the father of *all lies*, what truth does the devil want to cover up?

Let's Have a **Look . . .**

He wants to cover up the truth that *GOD IS REAL*. He wants to cover up the truth that *the Bible is God's Word*. He wants to cover up the truth that *Jesus Christ is God's son!*

> THIS IS GETTING GOOD!

That is the **Question. . .**

Can something be the truth and a lie?

Truth: Something that is real.

Lie: Something that is false.

Can something be the truth and a lie?

OF COURSE NOT!

NOW I MUST DECIDE

Choose for yourselves this day whom you will serve.

Joshua 24:15

I WANT TO KNOW THE TRUTH.

God is real. The Bible is God's word. Jesus Christ is God's Son. This is either the truth or a lie. It cannot be both.

You're **RiGHt ABOUt THAt!**

WE CAN KNOW THE TRUTH!

And *we must choose* who we will believe!

But the choice is easy.

Because *God is alive! And God is well!* His word is the truth. . .

Just **Think** About it!

And the truth of God's word will set us free!

This is **FREEDOM**

Not being a prisoner.

"If the Son sets you free, you will be free indeed."

John 8:36

Believe the Truth

In the beginning was the Word, and the Word was with God, and the Word was God.

John 1:1

WOW!

The Word *was* God! If this is true, and God is alive, then God's Word is alive, too!

But **WHAT IS GOD'S WORD?**

It's not *this* book. It's not any other book, either. God's written Word is the Bible. That's right! He said so Himself. . .and He ought to know.

For God Is the
Truth

God is not a man, that he should lie.
Numbers 23:19

That's right. . .
God cannot lie.
He is the truth.
And you can
believe the truth!

THAT'S A
GOOD CHOICE!

Now we
Know. . .

God is alive!
God's Word is alive!
God cannot lie!

We can believe
what God says!

THE TRUTH iS a PERSON!

I am the way and
the truth and the life.

John 14:6

THE TRUTH IS A PERSON!

What is the truth?
Is it a feeling? Is it an idea?
No! The Truth is a person.
In the Bible Jesus said, "I am
the way and the TRUTH
and the life."

What SHOULD I BELIEVE?

To know who to believe, I must want to know the truth. And Jesus is the truth! How do I get to know Him? The first step is easy. . .

And Here's the First Step

The first step is to pray. But what do we say when we pray? Here's a good way to begin:

Dear Jesus, if You are real, please show me. . . I want to know for sure.

AND HIS NAME IS JESUS CHRIST!

What is PRAYER?

When I talk to God with my own words, when I tell Him everything that's on my heart, I am praying. And He is listening!

I Can TRUST GOD'S WORD

All your words
are true.

Psalm 119:160

IT'S ALIVE!
IT'S ALIVE!

God's Word is alive.
We can trust everything it
says. And the Bible says
some amazing things! It says
God *loves* us. It says we can
live with Him *forever.*
It says Jesus wiped
all our sins away!

And THAT'S NOT ALL!

Good *does* love us. He wants the very best for us. And God's very best is found in His word. So we can trust Him and all He tells us there.

WELL, WOULD YOU LOOK AT THAT!

It's Time to Pray!

Dear Lord Jesus, I want to know You. I want to know Your word. Open my eyes, Lord. Open my heart. Fill me with truth. Make me just like You.

And I Quote...

For the word of God is living and active. . . .

Nothing in all creation is hidden from God's sight.

Hebrews 4:12–13

GOD'S LOVE

"I have loved
you with an
everlasting love."

Jeremiah 31:3

I THINK HE
MAY BE SERIOUS. . .

God loves us. He loves
us right now. Just the way
we are. He knows every good
thing about us. He knows
every bad thing, too. And He
loves us just the same.

How **can He Do That?**

JUST LISTEN TO THIS. . .

Why would God love us when He knows we've been bad? It's quite simple, really. Love is not something God does. Love is something He *is*!

Lord, Teach Me to
Pray. . .

Oh Lord, I want to know You. Open my eyes so I can see Your face. Open my heart and come make Your home here in me.

This is **Everlasting**

"Everlasting" means "forever."

When the sky and the stars are gone and forgotten, God will love us still. His love will last *forever*!

I WiLL NeVeR LeaVe YoU

*I will never leave you
nor forsake you!*

Joshua 1:5

HEY, WHERE DID
EVERYBODY GO?

God loves us. He will never
leave us. He will never, ever
forget to take care of us.
That is His promise. And
He will keep that promise. . .

forever!

And THAT'S A PROMISE!

No matter how bad things get, we are never alone. Even if everyone else in the whole world would choose to abandon us, God will still be there.

YOU KNOW WHAT THAT MEANS, DON'T YOU?

Lord, Teach Me to Pray...

Oh God, I know that You love me. I know You would never throw me away. People have hurt me. But I will forgive them. And I will turn and run to You.

REMEMBER this!

Here is something God will never do! He will never, ever take his love, his protection, or his help away from us. . .ever!

He Knows Me

> For you created
> my inmost being;
> you knit me together
> in my mother's womb.
>
> Psalm 139:13

YOU DID WHAT?!?

*G*od knew us long before we ever knew Him. His hands formed our bodies. His heart beats inside our own. Our lives, and the lives of *everything* around us. . .all these things exist because *He is alive.*

What **I AM,**
What I'm Not

Think about it! God *made* us. God *wants* us. We are not accidents. We are not mistakes. *We are miracles.*

I'M A MIRACLE!

Lord,
   Teach Me to
Pray...

Thank You God, for making me. And thank You for this life and all the good things in it. . . all these come from You!

Just listen to
THIS!

I praise you because I am fearfully and wonderfully made; your works are wonderful, I know that full well!

Psalm 139:14

OH YES HE can!

"*What is impossible with men is possible with God.*"

Luke 18:27

GOD CAN
DO WHAT?

God can do impossible things. He can make a blind man see. He can make a lame man dance. He can make a dead man come back to life!

Nothing is too hard for Him.

But **What About Me?**

There is nothing in this world so dead that God cannot bring it back to life again. Nothing. . . . *Nothing.*

Not even our hearts!

> GOD CAN DO ANYTHING!

Lord, Teach Me to **Pray . . .**

Dear Lord Jesus, here is my heart. I want to see what You see. I want to dance and be alive. Please make this darkness warm and clean and new again.

And I **Quote . . .**

"Let the little children come to me. . .for the kingdom of God belongs to such as these."

Jesus Christ,
Luke 18:16

FOREVER

> [The Lord] is good;
> His love endures forever.
>
> 2 Chronicles 5:13

FOREVER IS A LONG TIME!

There will never be a day when God does not love us. Things may go wrong. People may change. But God's love does not depend on people or things. It never has. It never will. *God is good.* And His love will last *forever!*

But **WHAT ABOUT TODAY?**

Jesus loves us *right now. . . just the way we are.* He will never give up on us. He will never stop loving us. That is His promise. We can trust it to be true.

YOU'RE RIGHT ABOUT THAT

Lord, Teach Me to **Pray. . .**

Oh Lord, You are good! Thank You for loving me. Thank You for being patient with me. Please teach me to be more like You.

What does **ENDURE** mean?

It means to keep on going, no matter how hard things are or how bad they get. And above all, to never, ever, *ever* give up!

HOPE

"Restrain your voice from weeping and your eyes from tears. . . . There is hope for your future, declares the Lord."

Jeremiah 31:16–17

I CERTAINLY HOPE SO!

Something good is about to happen! God says there is hope *for us.* Did something good happen today? Thank Him and accept His gift. Are you still waiting for something good to happen? *Thank Him. . .* and wait another day.

It's **HAPPENING RIGHT NOW!**

E very new day is a chance for God to do something amazing. *So trust Him! Expect something good.* Thank Him when He does it. Then trust Him to do it again!

I'M GOING TO TRUST GOD!

Lord, Teach Me to Pray. . .

T hank You Lord, for all the good things that have been a part of this day. Not one of these things would have ever been possible without You.

And I Quote. . .

"Everything is possible for him who believes!"

*Jesus Christ,
Mark 9:23*

EVERYTHING!

"*Everything is possible for him who believes!*"

Mark 9:23

I THINK I CAN. . .
I THINK I CAN. . .

"*Everything is possible for him who believes.*"

That's a beautiful thought.
And an amazing idea.
But do we really believe it?

Can WE REALLY BELIEVE IT. . .

And what if it's true? Do you know what that means? It means all we hope to do; everything we want to be; all of the deepest, *completely impossible* desires of our hearts. . .

All these are possible for those who believe!

Lord, Teach Me to Pray

I *believe you, Lord. You cannot lie. You will not lie. Everything is possible. Everything is possible! Everything is possible for him who believes!*

HE SAID I COULD! HE SAID I COULD!

And I Quote. . .

Now to him who is able to do. . .more than all we ask or imagine, according to his power that is at work within us, to him be glory. . .for ever and ever! Amen.

Ephesians 3:20–21

JUST BEAUTIFUL

For by him all things were created: things in heaven and on earth, visible and invisible.

Colossians 1:16

I'M NOT MAKING THIS STUFF UP, YOU KNOW!

It's a beautiful day today. The sun is shining. The air is clear and cool. The trees are wearing their leaves once again. Birds are singing. Flowers are blooming. What an amazing place this world is.

Just **THINK ABOUT IT!**

C an a flower be an accident? What about a star? How did all these beautiful things come to be? People say a lot of different things. What should I believe?

> THAT WOULD BE SOME ACCIDENT!

Lord, Teach Me to
Pray. . .

O h Lord, thank You for this beautiful day. Thank You for life and for this good world to live it in. And thank You for being the truth.

I'm just a little
THINKER. . .

Did God make the world? Or did the world make itself? Many people say the world *did* make itself— that everything is here by accident.

Can this be right?

45

SOMETHING GOOD

> In the beginning God created the heavens and the earth.
>
> *Genesis 1:1*

NOTHING COMES FROM NOTHING...

Think about it!

Did my house make itself?
Did my yard make itself?
Did my *lunch* make itself?
Did my *bed* make itself?

Can you think of anything that ever made itself starting out with nothing?

That's **A GOOD QUESTION!**

And if there isn't anything that made itself, then how did all these things come to be? That's right. . .

Somebody made them!

Lord, Teach Me to Pray. . .

Thank You, God, for making our world and everything in it.

> NOTHING EVER COULD!

That is the QUESTION. . .

How did the world begin?

Some people say a tiny ball of gas exploded in space and created everything. But if this is true, where did the tiny ball of gas come from, hmmm?

SOMETHING VERY GOOD

God saw all that he had made, and it was very good.

Genesis 1:31

I WOULD HAVE TO AGREE WITH YOU.

God saw all that he had made, and it was very good. This is either the truth or a lie. It can not be both! If it is a lie, we can ignore it.

But if it is the truth. . .

Then **GOD DID MAKE US!**

If it is the truth, then *God made us!* And when God saw what He had made (that would be us), *He said it was good. Very good!*

WELL, IT'S ABOUT TIME!

Lord, Teach Me to
Pray...

Oh Lord, thank You for creating me. Thank You for showing me the truth. I am not a mistake. I am not an accident. I am miracle made by Your own hands!

Now we're onto
SOMETHING...

How much does God love us? Listen to this:

For God so loved the world that he gave his one and only Son, that whoever believes in him shall not perish but have eternal life.

John 3:16

HE'S SEARCHING NOW

"For the Lord searches every heart and understands every motive."

1 Chronicles 28:9

IT'S TIME TO CHANGE.

God knows all about the bad things we've done. And He loves us anyway. But He knows those things can hurt us. So He wants us to change.

So **We Should Let Him**

Jesus wants to reach deep into our hearts. He wants to take out all the bad things. And then He wants us to throw those things away once and for all.

Lord, Teach Me to Pray...

Search me, Lord Jesus. Show me the things that are breaking Your heart. Bring them out in the open. Let me see them clearly. Then give me the courage to get rid of them for good.

CHANGE IS GOOD!

And I Quote...

Search me, O God, and know my heart. . . . See if there is any offensive way in me, and lead me in the way everlasting.

Psalm 139:23–24

WHat is FaitH?

The Lord is faithful to all his promises.

Psalm 145:13

FAITH IS THIS!

Faith is:

Believing what God says.

God wants us to trust Him. And we can trust Him. For Jesus loves us more than anyone ever did or could! He will never leave us. He will never forget us. God will keep every promise. We can believe what He says.

Wow! **DID YOU HEAR THAT?**

*T*he Lord is near to
all who call on him. . . .
He fulfills the desires
of those who fear him;
he hears their cry and
saves them.

Psalm 145:18-19

I SURE DID!

Lord, Teach Me to
Pray...

*J*esus, I know You are
here. You are here right
now. Please help me.
Help me to trust You.
Teach me to listen.
Let me hear Your voice.

I just want to be a
SHEEP. . . .

[Jesus said,] "I am the
good shepherd. . . . My sheep
listen to my voice. . . .
No one can snatch them
out of my Father's hand!"

John 10:14, 29

THIS IS FAITH

"[My sheep] will never follow a stranger; in fact, they will run away from him because they do not recognize a stranger's voice."

John 10:5

I LIKE BEING A SHEEP!

Faith is:
Listening to God's voice.

*G*od's voice is easy to hear. If we are listening, we will hear it. And it will sound like this:

"I have loved you with an everlasting love!"

That's **THE WORD OF GOD!**

That's right! God will speak to us by His Word. And God's written word is the Bible. Do we want to hear God's voice? *We should read the Bible!*

SHEEP CAN HEAR GOD'S VOICE!

Lord, Teach Me to Pray...

Thank You Lord for Your Word. Thank You for Your truth! Thank You for speaking to my heart. Help me to hear Your voice.

Who to Listen to...

This is God's voice:
"I will never leave you or forsake you."

And this is the stranger's:
"There is no God."

Have you heard the stranger's voice?

Run away!

ARe YOU talking to Me?

"What must I do
to be saved?"

Acts 16:30

YES, HE IS!

Life is good. If we
have a home, if we
have plenty of food to
eat, if we have friends
and families who love
us—what more could
anyone want?

Yes, **Its' a WONDERFUL LiFe**

And we're nice people, too! We go to church on Sunday. We work hard and try to help others. We've probably never hurt anyone. Why would we need to be "saved"?

MAN THE LIFEBOATS!

Lord, Teach Me to **Pray...**

Oh God, I just don't know what to do. . . . Do I really need to be "saved"? Isn't it enough to be a good person and go to church? Please show me Your way, and I will walk in it.

Danger, Danger, **DANGER!**

Your enemy the devil prowls around like a roaring lion looking for someone to devour.

1 Peter 5:8

Resist him!

saveD FROM WHat?

If we claim we have not sinned, we make [God] out to be a liar and his word has no place in our lives.

1 John 1:10

DANGER, DANGER, DANGER!

W hy do we need to be "saved"? And what do we need to be saved from?

Here's **WHAT THE BIBLE SAYS. . .**

If we claim to be without sin, we deceive ourselves and the truth is not in us.

1 John 1:8

> DON'T WORRY. . .
> HELP IS ON THE WAY!

Lord, Teach Me to *Pray. . .*

There's no reason to lie to myself any more. I have sinned! I know just what I've done. God knows, too. My sins have hurt my heart, and I want to be right again.

On the **SURFACE. . .**

My heart is a lot like a peaceful lake. . . . On the surface, everything can seem beautiful and calm. But God knows and can see *everything* that is lurking way down deep on the murky, unseen bottom.

I Have, too!

For all have sinned and fall short of the glory of God.

Romans 3:23

SOMEBODY OUGHT TO DO SOMETHING!

We are sinners. . .

But how can that be? We're a good people. . .we go to church. . .we've never, ever hurt anyone—not ever! Can we really be *sinners*?

Yes! For God says *all have sinned*. And that means we have sinned, too.

But DOES GOD STILL LOVE US?

Yes! God does love us. And He will never stop loving us. *But God hates sins. For sin can hurt— and will!*

SOMEBODY ALREADY HAS!

Lord, Teach Me to Pray...

Oh, Jesus, I'm so sorry. I am a sinner. And my sins are pushing You away. Please help me. Please show me what to do. Oh Lord, please take my sins away.

I am WHAT I AM...

I am a sinner. *And that is the truth.* I'm not proud of it. And I'm not quite sure how to change. But I do know this: Somehow, some way, God's truth is going to set me *free!*

WHaT to Do

> If we confess our sins,
> he is faithful and just
> and will forgive us our sins
> and purify us from all
> unrighteousness.
>
> *1 John 1:9*

BUT WHAT DO I DO NOW?

There's no use trying to hide it any more. . . *I have sinned.* And my sin is breaking God's heart. It's hurting me. It's hurting everyone around me. What can I do?

Please SHOW ME WHAT to Do...

And here's what to do!
If we confess our sins,
God will forgive us.
If we bring them out into
the open *where we both
can see them* and then
let go of them for good,
He will get rid of them
forever and we will never
see them again!

Lord, Teach Me to PRay... ❦ ❦ ❦

*Forgive me, Lord Jesus.
For I have sinned. Please
get rid of my sin and heal
my heart.*

> YOU RECEIVE
> HIS FORGIVENESS!

He completely
FoRGets...

"I. . .am he who blots out
your transgressions,
for my own sake, and
remembers your sins
no more."

Isaiah 43:25

The Final Word

Think About It!

*"I am the way and the truth and the life. No one comes to the Father except through me."**

- Can **ANYTHING** be the truth **AND** a lie?

- How many ways are there to God?

- How much does God love us?

- Why would Satan want to cover up the truth?

I Believe
The Truth...

- The devil is a liar. . .

- He is the father of ALL lies.

- The Truth is a PERSON. . .

- His name is Jesus Christ!

* Jesus Christ, John 14:6

Chapter Two

I BELIEVE JESUS!

The Bible says some amazing things!

. . .the Word was God!

GOD'S WORD IS ALIVE!

And I want to know if they are true. . .

Is the Bible just like any other book?

Or is it alive with the very life of Jesus Himself?

Now THAT would be **AMAZING!**

Let's Find out!

HE DiED FOR ME!

God demonstrates his love for us in this: While we were still sinners, Christ died for us.

Romans 5:8

HE LOVES ME LIKE THIS. . .

God loves us right now. He loves us *just the way we are.* We don't need to be perfect. We don't even need to get cleaned up first. His arms are open wide. All we have to do is come!

It's **okay, He can wait. . . .**

*G*od is not in a hurry. He knows we need to change. His love will change our hearts. But for now He just says, *"come. . ."*

Lord, Teach Me to **Pray...**

*T*hank You Lord, for forgiving my sins. Thank You for throwing them out for good. Help me to change. Thank You for Your love.

AND HE LOVES ME LIKE THIS!

Now is a good **Time. . .**

God knows what I have done. *He knows,* and He loves me anyway. He forgives the wrong things I've done when I ask Him to. So I will stop. *I will* ask Him to help me stop doing wrong things!

I AM FORGIVEN!

"I have swept away your offenses like a cloud, your sins like the morning mist. Return to me, for I have redeemed you!"

Isaiah 44:22

I AM A SINNER!

We all have sinned. And that's a fact. But now we know this truth as well: *We are forgiven. . . .* Yes, *we are forgiven!* And our sins will never be remembered again.

They're **GONE FOR GOOD**

God has washed them away. They are gone with the wind. Goodbye sins. . . goodbye *for good!* And thank You, Jesus. For *at last we are free!*

Lord, Teach Me to 𝒫ray. . .

Thank You, Lord Jesus. *Thank You for washing my sins away. Help me to start over. I want to begin again. I want to be like You.*

AND I AM FORGIVEN!!!

As I was Saying. . .

"Come now, let us reason together," says the Lord. "Though your sins are like scarlet, they shall be as white as snow."

Isaiah 1:18

COME UNTO ME!

"*Come to me,
all you who are
weary and burdened,
and I will
give you rest.*"

Matthew 11:28

I COULD USE SOME REST!

Jesus said, *"Come to me."* So that's just what we should do. We should lay down our anger. We should put away our sin. We should stop wasting time trying to figure everything out.

Let's let it all go, and just *come to Him!*

And I WiLL GiVe YoU Rest

*G*od loves us. We can trust Him. He will never leave us. He will never forget about us. Our lives are in His hands. *His hands made us.* And they will never let us go.

Lord, Teach Me to Pray...

*H*ere is my heart, Lord Jesus. Oh how I love You. Please take me and shape me into something beautiful and Holy and new.

LOOK OUT, JESUS, HERE I COME!

And I Quote...

"Come to me, all you who are weary and burdened. . . . Take my yoke upon you and learn from me, for I am gentle and humble in heart, and you will find rest for your souls. For my yoke is easy and my burden is light."

Matthew 11:28–30

73

use it all

But if. . .you seek the Lord your God, you will find him if you look for him with all your heart.

Deuteronomy 4:29

HE'S GOT TO BE AROUND HERE SOMEWHERE. . . .

If we've asked God to forgive us, there may be a strange, new feeling inside our hearts. We may not be sure what it is. But only one thing really matters now: We want to know Jesus! And we want to be with Him and be everything He wants us to be.

He's **in the secret place!**

But where is He? Where can we find Him? And how will we ever find Him if we don't know where to look?

Lord, Teach Me to
Pray...

Oh Lord, I want to know You. I want to be with You today. Please show me where You are, and I will come running to meet You there.

> YOU'RE GETTING WARMER. . .

"Seeking God"

God is not lost. He's right where He always has been. If we look for Him, we will find Him. And we will never be the same again!

BEHOLD...

I stand at the door and knock. If anyone hears my voice and opens the door, I will come in.

Revelation 3:20

KNOCK, KNOCK!

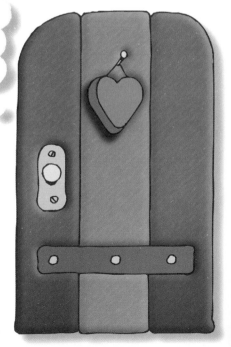

Jesus is standing at the door to our hearts. His voice is gently calling our names. Now is the time to open the door. Today is the day to let Him come in.

But **WHat IF WE'RE AFRaiD?**

Jesus loves us. He will not hurt us. He will not force us to open our hearts. He's knocking right now. But it's up to us to open the door and let His love in.

WHO'S THERE?

Lord, Teach Me to Pray...

Lord Jesus, here is my heart. Please come in. Come in today. Oh, Lord, please make my heart Your home. Help me not to sin any more.

Psomebody Psing me a

Psalm...

Create in me a pure heart, O God.

Psalm 51:10

WELCOME HOME!

... so that Christ may dwell in your hearts through faith.

Ephesians 3:17

HEY...THIS PLACE IS NICE!

Jesus lives inside of us. He lives inside our hearts. And Jesus is *big!* When He moved in, sin had to move out. And move out it did! At last we are clean! At last we are free! *Jesus is alive inside of our hearts!*

So That's What It Means!

And that is what it means to be born again. When Jesus comes to live in our hearts, His life is born into ours. And we are *born again!*

> I THINK I'M GOING TO LIKE IT HERE!

Lord, Teach Me to
Pray...

Thank You, Lord, for coming to live in my heart. Please sweep me clean of everything that would make me dirty again. I want to be fresh and clean and new.

The definition of:
Home...

What is a home?

It's the place where we are born. It's the place where we are loved. It's the place where we learn to live together. *It's the place where we belong.*

BORN AGAIN

"I tell you the truth, no one can see the kingdom of God unless he is born again."

John 3:3

HAPPY BIRTHDAY TO ME!

We have been born. . . again! God formed our bodies. He gave us life. He made us who we are. We grew inside our mothers' bodies until just the right time. And then "pop!" out we came.

We were born for the first time.

But **once is not enough!**

And we were alive! But something was missing. We could feel it deep down inside. We tried to fill the empty place with many different things. But when the fun of those things was gone, the emptiness was still there. *Why?*

Because I Must Be **Born Again!**

Only one thing is big enough to fill up the empty place in my heart. And that one thing is Jesus!

DOES THIS MEAN I GET TWICE AS MANY PRESENTS?!?

Home Again. . .

For my heart is meant to be God's home! And it is crying out for Him to come and live there with me.

So I will ask Jesus to come into my heart. And God will breathe *His life* into mine! Now Jesus is born in *me*. My heart is full. And I am complete. Jesus is home. I am *born again!*

CLEAN HOUSE!

...then, before the Lord, you will be clean from all your sins.

Leviticus 16:30

OOOUUCHH! WHO LEFT THAT THERE?!?

*I*t's time to clean house. Jesus is moving in, and this place is a mess!

Just DON'T GO in THERE...

Jesus wants to clean our house. And not just a few rooms, either... He wants to clean everything! Will I let Him into every room? Or are there still a few places I don't want Him to see?

IT'S TIME TO CLEAN IT GOOD!

Lord, Teach Me to Pray...

Here is my heart, Lord. Fill up every room. Shine Your light into every dark corner. You know what I'm hiding... Please help me to put it away.

What's that you're HIDING?

I'm not hiding anything! Honest! *I'm not!!!*

Am I?

BROKEN

> A bruised reed
> he will not break,
> and a smoldering wick
> he will not snuff out.
>
> *Matthew 12:20*

HELP ME, JESUS.

Did someone hurt you? That's terrible! Why would God let that happen? It's hard to know for sure. You may *never* really know why. And even though you've tried your best to forget, here you are. . .and the pain and the memory just won't go away.

Please **Tell Me Why!**

Jesus knows when we are bruised. He knows when we are broken. He will not snuff us out. We *will* live again. But for now we must wait. . . .

And we must forgive.

Lord, Teach Me to **Pray . . .**

Lord, I am bruised and broken. And I want to be angry forever. But You have forgiven me when I have broken and bruised others. And I will forgive those who have wounded me.

> HELP ME TO FORGIVE.

What about **Forgiveness. . .**

People will hurt me. But I will forgive. God forgave me. . . . *It cost Him His Son.*

PUNISH ME INSTEAD

He was pierced for our transgressions, he was crushed for our iniquities; the punishment that brought us peace was upon him, and by his wounds we are healed.

Isaiah 53:5

WHY WOULD HE DO A THING LIKE THAT?

*G*od loves us. But He hates our sin. Sin must be punished. And the punishment for sin is *death!* Did God punish us for our sin? No, He did not. Why? Because Jesus said, *"punish Me instead!"*

And **THAT'S JUST WHAT HE DID**

BECAUSE HE LOVES US, OF COURSE!

But that's not fair! Jesus never did anything wrong!

That's right. Jesus should not have died on the cross. *We should have.* But He took the punishment we deserved—the punishment we deserved for our sin.

Now when God looks at us, He *does not see our sin.* For our sin has been covered, and the price has been paid—paid for and covered by the blood of His Son.

That is how much God loves us. . . . We deserved to die. And to save us, He sacrificed His one and only Son so we could be set free!

But that's not **Fair. . .**

God did not give me what I deserve. I will never doubt His love again. Thank You, Jesus. Thank You for the cross. Thank You for saving me.

For the wages of sin is death.

Romans 6:23

87

He is Risen!

"I know that you are looking for Jesus, who was crucified. He is not here; he has risen, just as he said."

Matthew 28:6

NOW WE ARE SO HAPPY, WE DO THE DANCE OF JOY!

When Jesus died on the cross, our sins died right along with Him. Our "old" selves are dead. And they are buried for good!

But **It Doesn't End There. . .**

When Jesus rose from the grave, our "new" selves rose as well. *Jesus is alive.* And now we are alive and risen and free. . . *just like He is!*

Lord, Teach Me to
Pray ₀ ₀ ₀

Thank You, Lord, for a new beginning. The past is gone. And I can begin again. I will not look back. I will not turn around. You are calling me forward. And I will run to You!

STOP THAT! YOU'RE EMBARASSING ME!

What does
Alive mean?

Therefore, if anyone is in Christ, he is a new creation; the old has gone, the new has come!

2 Corinthians 5:17

Don't Look Back!

> But Lot's wife looked back. . . .
>
> *Genesis 19:26*

I DON'T WANT TO BE A PILLOW OF SALT!

The past is gone. And it's not coming back. *But that's good!* For Jesus does not want us to dig up our past.

And **I can DiG THat!**

NOT A *PILLOW OF SALT*. . . A *PILLAR OF SALT!*

WELL, I DON'T WANT TO BE THAT EITHER!

*O*ur old ways were hurting us. They had to be buried. If we try to dig them up, we will get stuck in the past— *and we will stay there forever!*

Lord, Teach Me to **Pray. . .**

*L*ord Jesus, my past belongs to You. I will not dig it up. I do not want it back. Please get rid of it. And turn my clean, new heart toward You.

He's working for my **GooD. . .**

God is *always* working for my good. If he has taken something away, then I will let it go. It must have been bad for me. . .*or He would not have taken it!*

WHY PRAY WHEN YOU CAN WORRY?

Cast all your anxiety on him because he cares for you.

1 Peter 5:7

WHY PRAY. . .

We love to worry. *We really do!* We worry about this; we worry about that. We worry we may forget to worry about something important. . . . We worry we might not be worrying about something we should really be very worried about.

Now I'M STARTING TO WORRY!

And that worries me!

But Jesus says *stop*! He wants us to gather up our worries and throw them all to Him.

But then we won't have anything to worry about! *What will we do with all our free time?*

Well. . .

Maybe I Could Pray. . .

Forgive me, Lord. I will stop worrying. I will learn to trust You. And I will learn to pray.

. . .WHEN YOU CAN WORRY?

Lord, teach me to

PRAY. . .

Am I worried? *I will pray!* Am I frightened? *I will pray!* Am I lonely? Angry? Confused? Troubled? Joyful? Jolly? Happy? Content? I will stop. . . . I will tell Jesus.

I will pray!

FOR MY GOOD

We know that in all things God works for the good of those who love him.

Romans 8:28

WELL, WHAT DO YOU KNOW. . .IT WORKED!

Some days are good. Some are bad. And the rest are just plain crazy! But Jesus loves us. He is taking care of us. And His promise is that *somehow* everything (yes, *everything*) will work out for our good.

And **THAT'S a PROMISE!**

We don't need to ask why.
We don't need to understand.
Jesus will take care of us.
Everything will be all right.

THAT'S GOOD!

Lord, Teach Me to Pray...

Oh, Lord, You are good.
And Your mercy will
go on forever and ever.
You will never leave me.
You will never forget me.
You are taking care of me.
Everything will be all right.

God will help me. I can **Wait. . .**

Jesus will fix the broken
things. I may have to wait
a little while. But I can do
that. *God will help me.* So
I will trust Him.

I will trust Him.
And I will wait.

DEEP

Then the angel showed me the river of the water of life, as clear as crystal, flowing from the throne of God.

Revelation 22:1

GO DEEP!

Jesus wants all of us. The water of His life runs clean and clear and pure. We can test it by dipping in our toes. And our toes will be glad that we did!

But there's just one problem. . .

That's **ONLY one part!**

Why should our toes have all the fun?

And do we really want to be dusty, dirty, and dried up when we can be cool and clean, sparkling clear and alive?

Lord, Teach Me to **Pray...**

Lord, Your water is deep. And I'm afraid I will drown. Please give me the courage to jump in all the way. I want to be clean and clear and entirely Yours.

> BUT I'M IN OVER MY HEAD ALREADY!

What God **Wants...**

What does God want?

God wants me! He is not angry. He will not hurt me. *Jesus loves me.* His water is cool. And I can come and drink until I am full.

HUMAN BEING OR HUMAN DOING?

How lovely is your dwelling place, O Lord!

Psalm 84:1

TO DO OR NOT TO DO. . .

Jesus loves us. We don't need to impress Him. We don't need to work to earn the love He gives for free. So the question is not *What does God want us to do? . . .*

Then **WHAT COULD IT BE?**

The question is *What does He want us to be?*

THAT IS THE PROBLEM!

Lord, Teach Me to
Pray. . .

Dear Jesus, please forgive me. I want to stop trying to earn Your love and just start obeying Your Word. Help me to put away my selfishness. Here I am, Lord. Teach me to be the person You want me to be.

Human Being. . .
OR HUMAN DOING?

What am I doing?
And why am I doing it?

Am I trying to earn God's love, or am I trying to be the person He wants me to be?

Be Still and Know!

> "Be still, and know that I am God."
>
> Psalm 46:10

HOOOWAAHABABAHOOO!

God knows what happened. He is not worried. He is not losing any sleep. But are we?

We need to *be still!*

So Be Still Already!

But how can we be still when everything around us is falling to pieces?

Everything around us is not falling to pieces. . . because God is not falling to pieces! So we will hold on to Him. And we will be still.

Lord, Teach Me to Pray . . .

Forgive me, Lord, for being worried. I know that You love me. You are God Almighty. And nothing is too hard or too big for You.

IIIIEEEEE OOOOOGA-OOOOGA! OOOOGA-BOOOOGAAA!!!

If it's good enough for the

Disciples . . .

Without warning, a furious storm came up on the lake. . . . But Jesus was sleeping. The disciples went and woke him, saying, "Lord, save us! We're going to drown!" He replied, "You of little faith, why are you so afraid?" Then he got up and rebuked the winds and the waves, and it was completely calm.

Matthew 8:24–26

ENOUGH FOR ME

The Lord is my shepherd,
I shall not be in want.

Psalm 23:1

THAT'S ENOUGH. . .

Jesus is taking good care of us. We will always have everything we need. He will not let us go hungry. *Jesus loves us.* There will always be enough.

And **ENOUGH IS ENOUGH!**

What do we really need? More clothes? More toys? More money? God doesn't promise to give us everything we want. He promises to give us everything we need.

THAT'S MORE THAN ENOUGH!

Lord, Teach Me to **Pray...**

Thank You, Lord, for taking care of me. I will not worry. I will trust You. You are my shepherd. Your hands already hold everything that I will ever need.

What's so great about a **SHEPHERD?**

Jesus is *my* shepherd. And I am His little sheep. So...

"If a man owns a hundred sheep, and one of them wanders away, will he not leave the ninety-nine... and go look for the one that wandered off? ... In the same way, your Father in heaven is not willing that any of these little ones should be lost."

Matthew 18:12, 14

103

I'M COMING APART!

> He makes me lie down
> in green pastures,
> he leads me beside
> quiet waters.
>
> Psalm 23:2

GO DOG, GO!

We love to *go, go, go* and *do, do, do*. And that's good! We live in an interesting world that God created. . .we are awake and alive with the new life of Christ!

Halt! **WHO GOES THERE?**

But if we never take time to stop and be with Jesus, all our busy *go, go, going* and *do, do, doing* will tear us apart.

Come Apart, or

Come Apart!

*G*od is not in a hurry.

He doesn't have somewhere to go. He doesn't have somewhere else He'd rather be. He has all the time in the world. And He wants to spend that time *with you!*

DO YOU LIKE MY HAT?

That's the
Secret place!

So I will stop. . . I will slip away from everyone and everything for just a while.

I will find a quiet place to be with God. And I will rest there and talk with Him today.

I WILL LET HIM

> He guides me in the paths of righteousness for his name's sake.
>
> Psalm 23:3

YOU WANT ME TO DO WHAT?!?

Where do we want to go today? What do we want to do? Sometimes it's hard to tell right from wrong. But Jesus is our shepherd. *If we let Him*, He will guide us. And our steps will always lead right to His side.

But **will we Let Him?**

I WANT YOU TO TRUST ME!

God's way may seem crazy. His path may look like a dead end. But we must learn to trust Him. Jesus can see what we can't. *And He is always working for our good.*

Lord, Teach Me to
Pray...

Dear Jesus, please teach me to trust You. Show me the right path, and I will take it. I want to be with You wherever you are.

FREEDOM...
in Jesus:

Jesus will show me what to do. *But He will never force me to do it!* God did not make me a puppet. He made me His child. I am alive. Jesus loves me. *And I am free!*

SHADOWS

Even though I walk through the valley of the shadow of death, I will fear no evil, for you are with me.

Psalm 23:4

DOWN IN THE VALLEY. . .

Everything has gone terribly wrong. My heart is broken. And I am afraid. I'm lost here in this dark valley. And the shadows are dark and long. When will things get better? When will I ever see the sun again?

The ONE THING ABOUT SHADOWS

I AM NOT ALONE!

Where there is no light, there can be no shadow. But when shadows are deep and black and dark and long, *somewhere* there must also be a bright light!

But Where Is the Light?

Are there shadows *in front of me? Then the light is behind me! Turn around! Turn away from the shadows! Now the darkness is gone. And I can see the light!*

Let there be LIGHT!

This is the way out of the valley! *Turn around!* Stop dwelling on the shadows! Turn and run!

Run toward God's light!

STOP!

Your rod and your staff, they comfort me.

Psalm 23:4

DID I DO THAT?

Jesus loves us. And because He does, He will correct us when we're wrong. We don't like to be corrected. But Jesus knows what's best for us. And sometimes He must say *stop!*

And **NOW IS THE TIME**

Is something hurting us? Are we hurting someone else? It's time to stop. It's time to say *I'm sorry.*

> WELL, IT SURE WASN'T ME!

Teach Me to **Pray . . .**

Forgive me, Lord. I have wandered away from You. My sins set a trap for me. They told me to run away and hide from You. I listened to them. And now I am lost again. Please come and find me. I want to come back home.

Please tell me **WHAT TO DO. . .**

Do not lie. . . . Do not steal. . . . Love your enemy. . . . Pray for the person who hurts you. . . . Give, and do not expect to get anything in return!

God's Word will tell us exactly what to do. *But it's up to us to listen.*

THE ODD COUPLE

You prepare a table before me in the presence of my enemies.

Psalm 23:5

SUPPERTIME!

We may not like certain people. And those people may not like us either! But when Jesus is alive inside of our hearts, our hearts must not make war with *anyone* anymore. Jesus died for us. *Jesus died for others, too.* God will help us. We will have peace.

The **way to COOL OFF. . .**

$\mathring{A}$nger is the fuel that powers a fight. Is my friend trying to make me angry? I will not add fuel to his fire. I will stop the fight before it starts—*with the love of Jesus Christ!*

Lord, Teach Me to *Pray...*

$\mathring{O}$h, Lord, please help me deal with my angry friend. I don't need to fight. I won't try to get even. Please bring us Your peace.

And I Quote. . .

A gentle answer turns away wrath, but a harsh word stirs up anger.

Proverbs 15:1

ALL THE TIME!

You anoint my head with oil; my cup overflows.

Psalm 23:5

I SURE WASN'T EXPECTING THIS!

God is good. *All the time!* Everywhere we look we see the beautiful, living proof of all the good things He does for us. We can feel Him in our hearts. We can touch Him with our prayers. We can hear Him in the Word.

And **THAT IS THE TRUTH!**

I know we don't deserve it. But we have it just the same. He has given us life. And all of the wonderful things in our world live and move and exist because of Him!

Lord, Teach Me to Pray...

Thank You, Jesus, for this life You've given me. Thank You for saving me and making me whole. Thank You for all the good things that have come from Your hands. And thank You for the cross. I love You, Jesus. I love You. Thank You, Lord, for loving me.

HEY, BE CAREFUL! YOU'RE SPILLING IT EVERYWHERE!

And forever is a long **TIME!**

Give thanks to the Lord, for he is good. His love endures forever!

Psalm 136:1

115

F✺REVER

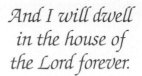

> *And I will dwell in the house of the Lord forever.*
>
> *Psalm 23:6*

FOREVER IS A LONG TIME!

*O*ne day our lives on this earth will end. Our bodies will die. *But we will live!* We will step into the glorious light of heaven, where at last we'll be with Him.

And **THAT'S WHERE I BELONG!**

This world has never been our home. *For we are alive with the life of Christ Himself.* He knows us each by name. And one day He will call us home.

AND WE WILL LIVE WITH HIM—FOREVER!

Lord, Teach Me to **Pray . . .**

Thank You, Lord, for the cross of Jesus Christ. Thank You for washing all my sins away. Make my life a blessing while I am here on the earth. Lord, I am waiting here for You.

Yes, I am coming **Soon. . .**

"Behold, I am coming soon! Blessed are those who wash their robes, that they may have the right to the tree of life and may go through the gates into the city."

Revelation 22:12, 14

Let it SHine!

"No one lights a lamp and hides it in a jar."

Luke 8:16

HAS ANYONE SEEN MY FLASHLIGHT?!?

*O*ur friends need the light that God's Word can bring. Are we shining the love of Jesus into their lives? Or are we hiding it under the covers and keeping it all to ourselves?

What WILL PEOPLE THINK?

It can be a little bit scary to talk about Jesus with our friends. We don't want everyone to think we're crazy. *Even if we are!* But very often those fears are just plain wrong. . . .

Surprise, Surprise, Surprise!

And when we open up and begin to share, we find that our friends actually want to hear what we have to say!

So don't be afraid. . . Share the good news with someone else.

Do it today!

THIS LITTLE LIGHT OF MINE. . . I'M GONNA LET IT SHINE!!!

As I was Saying. . .

"No one lights a lamp and hides it in a jar or puts it under a bed. Instead he puts it on a stand, so that those who come in can see the light."

Luke 8:16

I can Fix tHat!

"Why do you look at the speck of sawdust in your brother's eye and pay no attention to the plank in your own eye?"

Matthew 7:3

BROTHER, I KNOW JUST WHAT YOU NEED!

My friend is wrong. *Wrong, wrong, wrong!* Why can't he see it? It's as plain as the nose on his face! Someone needs to fix him. And it might as well be me. . .

Right?

It **HaD tø Be Yøu. . .**

Wrong! There's only one person *in the whole world* that I can fix. And that one person *is me.* *And only you can fix you.*

Talk about Your

Fixer-Upper!

Jesus said love one another. *But He did not say* fix *one another. Fixing is God's work. And He can do it without hurting. But we cannot. So let's stop trying to fix. And let's start trying to love.*

SIGH. . .

A good place to

Start. . .

Be kind and compassionate to one another, forgiving each other, just as in Christ God forgave you.

Ephesians 4:32

No More Mr. Nice Guy

Love must be sincere.

Romans 12:9

ALL I SAID WAS
"HOW ARE YOU?"

We can be nice!
we can smile and say
hello. We can promise
to drop by soon. We
can listen and pretend
to be concerned. . .

*But do we mean the
things we say and do?*

Can **I Get an Amen?**

It's time to stop being nice! It's time to start being real. Our friends need help. They need a love with hands and feet. They need a friend who speaks the truth. So let's stop pretending. And let's help our friends for real.

I DIDN'T ACTUALLY WANT YOU TO TELL ME!

Lord, Teach Me to **Pray...**

Forgive me, Lord, for pretending. Please make my love alive and real and true like Yours.

What is a true **FRIEND?**

Do I have a true friend? *That is a great gift!* Am I a true friend to someone else? *That is part of what it means to be a Christian.*

123

I BELIEVE JESUS!

I am not ashamed, because I know whom I have believed.

2 Timothy 1:12

YOU CAN SAY THAT AGAIN!

𝒫eople will make fun of us for believing Jesus. But that's okay. Deep in their hearts they know Jesus is right. *And they are afraid. . . .*

So let's speak the truth. And then let's pray. Jesus changed our hearts. He can change their hearts, too.

But **WHO can It Be?**

The truth is a person. And He is alive and well —*right here in our hearts!*

We know who to believe. . . . *We believe Jesus!*

I BELIEVE JESUS!!!

Lord, Teach Me to **Pray**. . .

Jesus, You are The Truth. I can know You. I can trust You. You are real. And You love me. You will show me what to do. You will tell me who to believe. So I will listen for Your voice. And I will follow You.

So I'll say it **Again**. . .

People love to talk. They say a lot of different things. Some of those things are right. And some are just plain wrong. But now I know the difference. . .

Because I know the truth!

IN THE DARK

> The Lord turns my
> darkness into light.
>
> 2 Samuel 22:29

LET THERE BE LIGHT!

Yesterday was beautiful
and warm. And we were
happy. But something has
changed. Suddenly it's windy
and cold. The darkness is
falling. And we can't see
God anymore.

But that's okay. . . . We know
He's still here. *And we know
that He loves us.*

Right **WHERE YOU LEFT ME**

You did not leave us in the dark. . . .

You left us in the light!

And the Light Is God's Word!

So I will run to You, Lord Jesus. And I will see the light again. For You are the Living Word the beautiful, blinding, holy light of this fallen world. Darkness cannot survive in Your presence.

And I cannot survive without You!

AT LAST I CAN SEE!!!

What is the LIGHT?

Your word is a lamp to my feet and a light for my path.

Psalm 119:105

POUR it THROUGH the WORD

Dear friends, do not believe every spirit, but test the spirits to see whether they are from God.

1 John 4:1

THIS COULD GET A BIT MESSY!

Did God say it? *Then we can believe it.* But everything else we hear must be tested by His Word.

And here is the test: Does it agree completely with the Bible? *Then we can keep it.* Is it different in any way? *Then we can throw it away— and we should!*

That's **one TOUGH TEST!**

That's right! But if God's Word is the truth, then *anything that does not agree with it must be a lie!*

Just a Gentle Reminder...

When we hear something that does not agree with God's Word, we don't ever have to wonder where it came from. . . . We can be sure that it slithered right out of Satan's very own nest. *"There is no truth in him."*

[The devil] is a liar and the father of lies!

John 8:44

AND THAT IS THE TRUTH!

If the Son sets you free, you are
FREE INDEED!

I run in the path of your commands, for you have set my heart free!

Psalm 119:32

I REFUSE TO WORRY

Do not let
your hearts
be troubled.

John 14:1

WHAT MAKES YOU
THINK I'M WORRIED?

Let's refuse to worry. *God is in control.* Nothing can surprise Him. Nothing can make Him forget about us. Our lives are in His hands. And His hands are big enough and strong enough to handle *anything.*

And **THAT IS a PROMISE!**

Jesus promised to provide for all our needs. Can you think of even *one day* when this promise did not come true?

Lord, Teach Me to Pray...

Lord, please forgive me. You always give me everything I need. I will stop worrying about all the crazy things going on around me. You know what to do. So I will be still. And I will look to You.

I CAN'T EVEN THINK OF ONE!

How to get old QUICK...

Worry is a thief. It will take this good day God made just for me and throw it right into the trash. . .if I let it!

Who of you by worrying can add a single hour to his life?

Matthew 6:27

LOOK UP!

MAN, WHAT A LIFE!

Do birds worry?

Do birds worry? *Of course not!* They're too busy flitting and flapping and *singing for joy* over all of the wonderful, incredible blessings God has given and the amazing, beautiful, good, green world He created just for them!

Okay, **I get the point!**

WHERE DO I SIGN UP?

Why should we worry? Just give me one good reason! Jesus loves us. He will take care of us. We will *always* have everything we need.

Lord, Teach Me to Pray...

Thank You, Jesus! Thank You for flowers and trees and sunshine and cool water and all of the good things You've done for me! Thank You for loving me. Thank You for taking care of me. Teach me to see and to sing and be glad!

Sing for JOY!

Shout with joy to God, all the earth! Sing the glory of his name; make his praise glorious!

Psalm 66:1–2

133

MADE IN THE SHADE!

I delight to sit in his shade, and his fruit is sweet to my taste.

Song of Solomon 2:3

THANK YOU, JESUS!

What a beautiful day. The sun is singing its silvery golden song. The air is crisp and clean and cool. And here we are in the Secret Place. . . .

Lord, **HERE IS MY HEART. . .**

OH, HOW I LOVE YOU!

So teach us, oh Lord.
Open up our hearts.
Fill us with Your spirit.
We are not in a hurry. . . .
We just want to be with
You today.

Lord, Teach Me to
Pray. . .

*Thank You, Lord, for
this quiet, Secret Place.
Oh, how I love You! Fill
up my spirit with Your
goodness. Light up my
heart with Your Word.
Bless my small feet with
Your awesome, mighty
courage. Open my hands
and let them pour out
Your love.*

Think on these
THINGS. . .

Do not be afraid, little
flock, for your Father
has been pleased to
give you the kingdom.

Luke 12:32

peace

And the peace of God, which transcends all understanding, will guard your hearts and your minds in Christ Jesus.

Philippians 4:7

HERE IS MY HEART, LORD. . . .

There is no reason to worry. God is working everything out for our good. So let's thank Him for His kindness. And let's share our hearts with Him.

Let's **Take a Peek Inside**

Now Jesus can flood us with His peace. And our worries and concerns will be washed clean away by the power of His love.

Lord, Teach Me to **Pray. . .**

Thank You, Lord, for Your peace. Thank You for guarding my heart. I know that You love me. And I know I can trust You. I don't ever need to worry. Things will work out fine.

THANK YOU FOR YOUR PEACE!

And I **Quote. . .**

Do not be anxious about anything, but in everything, by prayer and petition, with thanksgiving, present your requests to God.

Philippians 4:6

On GuaRD!

And the peace of God, which transcends all understanding, will guard your hearts and your minds in Christ Jesus.

Philippians 4:7

HALT!

Jesus is guarding the door to our hearts. He is guarding it *with His peace.* Nothing will ever get past Him. No one is big enough to push Him aside. He is watching over us. And we are safe.

Watch WHERE YOU STAND!

WHO GOES THERE?

Do we trust what Jesus says? *Then our armor will be peace.*

Are we worried and afraid? We have stepped in front of Jesus. We have taken off our armor. And now *Satan can attack!*

Lord, Teach Me to
Pray. . .

Thank You, Lord, for guarding my heart. Thank You for taking care of me. Who could ever hope to harm me when You stand here at my door?

What does it mean to
GUARD?

1. To protect from danger or harm.

2. To control who or what may pass through an entrance or across a border.

PRAY WITHOUT CEASING!

Pray
continually.

1 Thessalonians 5:17

PRAY WITHOUT
SNEEZING?

God's Word says *pray continually*. And *continually* means without stopping! But how in the world are we supposed to do that?

It's **Really Quite Simple**

What is prayer? Is it reading beautiful words from a book? Is it repeating a few special phrases at just the right time? Is it whispering a quick "bless me" before we jump into our beds?

Those things can be prayer when they come from the heart. But the kind of prayer God longs to hear is really quite a bit different than that. . . .

Prayer is TALKING!!!

Prayer is simply talking to Jesus! And we can do that anytime—or anywhere. So we will! We will start talking to Jesus from our hearts. And we will never, ever stop!

HOW IN THE WORLD ARE WE SUPPOSED TO DO THAT?

What's so great about

Prayer?

We can tell Jesus anything.

It doesn't matter where I am or what I'm doing. . . He will hear me. He will not get angry. He will not make fun of me. Jesus loves me.

I can talk to Him.

HELP iS on THE WaY!

*Before they call
I will answer; while
they are still speaking
I will hear.*

Isaiah 65:24

HOW LONG,
OH LORD?!?

Jesus hears us when
we pray. And His answer
will come. It may come today. It may come tomorrow.
Or I might have to wait
for a very long time. But
Jesus loves us. And He knows
what we need. So we will
wait. His answer *will* come.

How DID He Know That?

It's not easy to wait. And it isn't any fun either. But waiting can be part of God's answer to our prayers. If we slow down and hang on, God will surely come. His answer may not be what we expected. . .*but it will be amazing!*

BE PATIENT, MY CHILD!

Lord, Teach Me to Pray. . .

Thank You, Jesus, for hearing my prayer. I never expected You to do anything like this. But now I see that You were right. And I rejoice in the answer You have provided.

That's not what I

EXPECTED. . .

Jesus may do what we expect Him to. And He may not. But He is God. . . .

And we are not!

ARID. . .and EXTRA DRY!

"Son of man, can these bones live?"

Ezekiel 37:3

THIS PUPPY IS DRY!

Jesus can change *anyone's* heart. Nothing is too hard for Him. No one is too far gone. No matter how hopeless they seem to be. . .

Jesus can change any heart!

So **PRaY ALReaDY!**

*O*ur friends can ignore our words. They can stop us cold every time we try to help. They can tie our hands or seal up our lips. . . .

But they are helpless against our prayers!

THIS PUPPY IS BONE DRY!

Lord, Teach Me to

Pray . . .

*L*ord, thank You for my friend. She is mixed up and angry. But I love her. And I want her to know You like I do. Please come and change her heart.

Thus says the

LoRD. . .

"Dry bones, hear the word of the LORD. . . . I will put breath in you, and you will come to life. . . . I will put my Spirit in you and you will live."

Ezekiel 37:4, 6, and 14

THAT I MAY KNOW YOU

"Teach me your ways so I may know you."

Exodus 33:13

IS THAT YOUR FINAL ANSWER?

Jesus is changing everything. And that's good! But we may still have so many questions. And there may be many things we just don't understand. . . .

I THINK I NEED a LIFELINE. . .

WHAT WAS THE QUESTION AGAIN?

But when the time is right, Jesus will open His hands. All of our answers are waiting there for us. . . . So let's be patient. And let's pray. Don't get in a hurry. Our lives, and everything in them, belong to Him.

Teach Me to Pray. . .

Lord Jesus, here is my heart. Mold me and make me into something beautiful and clean and new. Fill me with Your Spirit. Shape me with the gentle hand of Your Word. Teach me not to hurry. I want to be like You.

So BiG!

Some questions never get answered. And some answers only lead to more questions! But Jesus loves me. And I want to know Him. So I will bring Him my questions. . . .

And He will give me His heart.

The Final Word

Think About It!

In the beginning was the Word, and the Word was with God, and the Word was God.*

- If God is the Truth, can His Word be a lie?

- Would God send His son to die **FOR US** if our lives were nothing but **accidents**?

- If God made **EVERYTHING** that is or **EVER WAS**, what problem could possibly be too big for Him to solve?

I Believe
The Truth...

- God's Word is ALIVE!

- I can believe what God says.

- Jesus LOVES me!

- His death washed my sin away.

John 1:1

Chapter Three

A Love Like God's

Jesus loves me.
I know that for sure!
His love is changing
everything. . . .

I want to walk
and talk and live
and breathe the
amazing new life
He's given to me.

I don't just
want to SAY
that I'm
a believer.

I want to BE
one for REAL. . . .

But

HOW Do I

DO IT?

Let's
FiND OUT!

GOD'S SECRET PLACE

He who dwells in the [Secret Place] of the Most High will rest in the shadow of the Almighty.

Psalm 91:1

NO ONE WILL EVER FIND ME HERE!

It's a beautiful morning. The air is clear and cool. Our hearts are quiet and still. And Jesus is here. So let's open up our Bibles. And let's open up our hearts.

Where **Do I Live?**

There's no need to hurry. This is where we belong. Jesus is here. He's here right now. *We have found God's Secret Place!*

NO ONE BUT JESUS!

Lord, Teach Me to **Pray...**

Thank You, Lord Jesus, for meeting me here. Thank You for making my heart Your home. I want to be with You more than anything else in this world.

What does **DWELLING** mean?

Does Jesus live in my heart? Has He made my heart His home?

Then Jesus dwells— *He lives*—in me. He isn't just visiting. He's come to stay!

153

THERE'S NO PLACE LIKE HOME!

Don't you know that you yourselves are God's temple and that God's Spirit lives in you?

1 Corinthians 3:16

THERE'S NO PLACE LIKE HOME. . .

Jesus is alive inside of our hearts. He's made our hearts His home. But what about us? Do we live each moment of our days with Him? Or do we just drop by now and then to say hello?

Well HOW DO YOU DO?

When we move in and make ourselves at home with Him, God promises to keep us safe and give us every good thing that we will ever need!

...EXCEPT GRANDMA'S!

Lord, Teach Me to Pray...

Good morning, Lord Jesus. Here I am again today. And there is no place else I'd rather be than right here with You.

And I Quote...

If you make the Most High your dwelling. . .then no harm will befall you.

"Because he loves me," says the Lord, "I will rescue him. . .and show him my salvation!"

Psalm 91:9, 10, 14, and 16

155

TO BOLDLY GO. . .

Let us then approach the throne of grace with confidence.

Hebrews 4:16

WE NEED MORE POWER!

God's Word says be bold. *So let's be bold!* Let's come to Jesus with reckless, ridiculous confidence because we know *for certain* He hears every word we pray and will answer us when we call upon His name!

A Strange, New World!

Jesus wants to talk to us! We are not bothering Him when we pray. He is never too busy to listen to what we have to say. He is waiting for us *right now*. So we will come and pour our hearts out to Him.

That's What the Man

SAID!

"Is anything too hard for the Lord?"

Genesis 18:14

BEAM ME UP!

How do I come to God BOLDLY?

The Bible says come to Jesus with fearless daring, without modesty or make-believe, ready and willing for the greatest adventure that we will ever know!

I can HeaR You!

> If we ask anything according to his will, he hears us. And if we know that he hears us. . . we know that we have what we asked of him.
>
> *1 John 5:14–15*

OKAY. . .LET ME HAVE IT!

Jesus hears us when we pray. And we can ask Him for anything. . .anything at all!

Will we get what we want? Well, that depends. . .

Anything MY Heart Desires

Jesus can give us the desires of our hearts. And He will. . .when we allow the desires of our hearts to be blown away and replaced by the desires of His heart.

WELL, YOU ASKED FOR IT. . .

Lord, Teach Me to Pray. . .

Lord, You know the one thing I want more than anything else in the whole world. Please take it away. Put Jesus in its place. Thank You, Lord. . . . Now I have everything that I will ever need.

The rest of the Story. . .

This is the confidence we have in approaching God: that if we ask anything according to his will, he hears us. And if we know that he hears us—whatever we ask—we know that we have what we asked of him.

1 John 5:14–15

THaT'S IMPOSSiBLe!

"Nothing is impossible with God."

Luke 1:37

I AM THE LORD'S SERVANT!

Nothing is impossible
with God. *Nothing at all!*
No mountain is too big.
No problem is too hard.
It's never too late. And
no one is ever too far gone.

So let's trust Him. And let's
see all that God can do.
He will do the impossible. . . .
He will do it today!

I'll **Say It Again...**

MAY IT BE TO ME AS YOU HAVE SAID!

"*Is anything too hard for the Lord?*"

Genesis 18:14

Lord, Teach Me to *Pray...*

Thank You, Lord Jesus. Thank You for loving me. Please forgive me for thinking that You do not care. You are not small and weak and far away. You are God Almighty. And You will make a way. Nothing is too hard for You.

I tell you the **TRUTH...**

"I tell you the truth, if you have faith as small as a mustard seed, you can say to this mountain, 'Move from here to there' and it will move. Nothing will be impossible for you."

Matthew 17:20–21

How to Move a Mountain

"If you have faith as small as a mustard seed, you can say to this mountain, 'Move from here to there' and it will move."

Matthew 17:20

YODEL AAAY HEE HOOO!

How can we ever hope to move this mountain? *It is enormous!* And its shadows are dark and long.

And THAT'S THE TRUTH!

But Jesus said, "It will move." So yes, *He can move it. And it will disappear.* But before that can happen, there's one simple thing we must do *by ourselves. . . .*

And Here's What it is!

WHAT MUST I DO?

We must turn around! *We must stop looking at the mountain and look at Jesus instead.*

Did you turn around? Now the mountain is not standing in your way. You are free! And you can see Jesus once again.

What faith does to Mountains. . .

I will lay waste to the mountains and hills. . . I will turn the darkness into light before them and make the rough places smooth.

Isaiah 42:15–6

MORE THAN ENOUGH

And the jug of oil did not run dry.

1 Kings 17:16

WILL HE GIVE ME A PUPPY?

Jesus loves us. He will not forget about us. We don't ever have to worry. He will give us everything we need.

That's **JUST THE WAY HE IS!**

Has your bottle run dry? He will open a new one! Have the doors all slammed shut? He will throw open the windows! There will always be enough...
when we are trusting in Him!

Lord, Teach Me to **Pray...**

Thank You, Jesus, for taking care of me. There has never been even one single day when You forgot about me. I know that You love me. And I can trust You for everything I need today.

DO YOU NEED A PUPPY?

That is the **Question...**

Was it a miracle?

Was it a miracle that the widow's jug of oil did not run dry? *You bet it was!* Is it wrong to expect Jesus to do the same thing for me today? *Of course not!*

Miracles are a normal, everyday way that God works. *And He will do them for us!*

Sing!

*I will sing
to the Lord,
for he has been
good to me.*

Psalm 13:6

**JESUS LOVES
BAD SINGING!**

God loves singing!
He loves good singing.
He loves bad singing.
So sing! Sing to the
Lord! Tell Him that you
love Him. Tell Him that
you need Him. Thank
Him for His goodness.
Sing to the Lord today!

And **IT'S A GOOD THING!**

Why would God want us to sing? Who knows? But He says it over and over and over again. *So sing we should!* Good, bad, or just plain ugly. . .let's lift up our voices. And let's worship Him!

AND IT DOESN'T GET ANY WORSE THAN THIS!

Lord, Teach Me to **Pray. . .**

Thank You, Lord, for the voice You gave me. I will use it today to sing Your praise!

As I was **Saying. . .**

Sing to the Lord, you saints of his.
Psalm 30:4

Sing praises to God.
Psalm 47:6

Sing and make music in your heart.
Ephesians 5:19

Sing of the Lord's great love.
Psalm 89:1

PLUMB AND TRUE!

Then the Lord said, "Look, I am setting a plumb line among my people."

Amos 7:8

PLUMB MEANS STRAIGHT!

Do not lie. Do not steal. Do not kill. . . . It is no secret what God wants us to do. His commandments are plain and simple. And we know just what they mean.

But like a builder's plumb line, God's commands do not make us straight. They only show us where we are crooked!

It's **OKAY TO BE CROOKED. . .**

AND STRAIGHT IS GREAT!

But because God loves us, He is not about to leave us that way.

God gave us our lives. We may have bent them and broken them and messed them all up. But that's all right. The hands that made us can put us back together. . . .

So let's run into His arms. Let's tell Him what we've done. God will forgive us. Jesus loves us. Today let's give Him our hearts.

What is a **PLUMB Line?**

A plumb line is a string with a weight at one end used by a builder to check his work to be sure it is standing perfectly straight.

WHAT. . .ME WORRY?

Do not worry about your life.

Matthew 6:25

HABAHABAHABAHABA. . .

We know that God loves us. We know He hears us when we pray. He is bigger and stronger than anything that will ever come against us. And He will supply all of our needs.

So why do we worry?

Our **Father Knows Best**

Do we really think God does not care about us? *Or are we afraid He may not let us have our own way?*

STOP THAT. . .YOU'RE MAKING ME NERVOUS!

Lord, Teach Me to **Pray . . .**

Jesus, please forgive me. I am worried about everything. And I want to stop. Please take away all my worries. And give me the things that You know I need.

I Did It **His way. . .**

God knows what will happen tomorrow. And He is working everything out for my good. Nothing will ever take Him by surprise. So I will trust Him. *And I will relax. . .* and then follow Him wherever He goes.

I Can Hear You

" 'Speak, Lord, for your servant is listening.' "

1 Samuel 3:9

DID YOU HEAR THAT?

Do we want to hear God's voice? Then we must be quiet! If God needs to shout to get our attention, we are not really listening for Him.

Not in the Whirlwind

Then a great and powerful wind tore the mountains apart... but the Lord was not in the wind.

After the wind there was an earthquake, but the Lord was not in the earthquake.

After the earthquake came a fire, but the Lord was not in the fire.

And after the fire came a gentle whisper. . . Then a voice said to him, "What are you doing here, Elijah?"

1 Kings 19:11-13

WHAT!?! HUH??? DID YOU SAY SOMETHING?

Through His WORD. . .

What does God's voice sound like? How will I know when I hear it? Just listen to this!

The Lord continued to appear at Shiloh, and there he revealed himself to Samuel **through his word**.

1 Samuel 3:21

Still. . .

"Be still, and know that I am God."

Psalm 46:10

HAVE YOUR PEOPLE CALL MY PEOPLE AND WE'LL DO LUNCH!

Do we want to hear God's voice? *Then we must be still!* God can speak to us any time. He can speak to me anywhere. . . .

But if we're always busy with something or someone else, *how will we ever hear Him?*

That's **WHAT I HEARD...**

Are you loud and fast and busy? You will only hear yourself.

Are you still? *That is when you can hear God's voice!*

Lord, Teach Me to
Pray...

Oh, Lord, I want to hear Your gentle voice once more. Please help me to slow down and turn off the noise all around me. I want to be with You today.

> **BUT I DON'T HAVE ANY PEOPLE!**

I can hear His
Voice...

God *may* speak in a voice I can hear with my ears. He *may* speak with a voice I can hear in my heart. But God will speak. And I will hear His voice. . . . *When I open my Bible and meet with Him there.*

GENTLY!

> Brothers, if someone is caught in a sin, you who are spiritual should restore him gently.
>
> *Galatians 6:1*

HELP! I'VE FALLEN AND I CAN'T GET UP!

*O*ur friends can make some terrible mistakes. They hurt themselves. They hurt everyone around them, too. We want to help. But we may not know exactly what to do.

Where **Do** we start?

Sin is like a trap. Its sharp, rusty teeth will snap shut on our hearts and hold us in one spot until we die.

Are our friends caught in the trap of sin? Then they are hurt! They do not need a sermon. They need a friend.

Lord, Teach Me to **Pray. . .**

Lord, I want to help my friend. Please show me the way to set her free.

> IS ANYBODY LISTENING?

There's still time to CHANGE. . .

My friend has sinned. . . . But what did I do? Did I turn my back on her? Did I tell her to go away?

Now I have sinned, too.

177

I FORGIVE YOU

Forgive whatever grievances you may have against one another.

Colossians 3:13

I FORGIVE YOU.

Jesus forgave us. So we must forgive our friends. Yes, they are sometimes wrong. But we have been wrong, too. And we are sorry. But there is still time to forgive others. *So let's forgive them.* And let's ask them to forgive us.

Let's do it *today*.

The **DeVil IS a LiaR...**

The devil wants us to hate and be angry. And he will whisper, *"You can never forgive that!"* But the devil is a liar. And he's stupid, too.

We *can* forgive.
And we should.

Teach Me to **Pray...**

Jesus, I forgive the one who hurt me so much. Today I take the memory of all that happened and give it up to You. Please take it far away. I don't ever want it back. I forgive them, Lord Jesus. At last I am free!

YOU DO?

Sin and **Bear it...**

Bear with each other and forgive whatever grievances you may have against one another. Forgive as the Lord forgave you.

Colossians 3:13

STOMP ON THE DEVIL!

If I had cherished sin in my heart, the Lord would not have listened.

Psalm 66:18

I HAD NO IDEA IT WAS THIS EASY!

Sin will separate us from God. *And the devil knows it!* He knows that when we hate our friends and refuse to forgive them, God will not hear our prayers.

So **TURN ON THE LIGHTS!**

But when we truly forgive others the way Jesus forgave us, the devil's hold on me is broken. For Satan cannot stand the presence of God. And when we forgive, *God's presence floods in from everywhere and pours out of everything!*

YES, I FORGIVE YOU!!!

Lord, Teach Me to
Pray . . .

Thank You, Lord, for the cross. Thank You for washing my sins away. I love You Jesus. And because of You I can forgive my friend.

Now here's the rest of the
Story. . .

But God has surely listened and heard my voice in prayer. Praise be to God, who has not rejected my prayer or withheld his love from me!

Psalm 66:19–20

DO YOU LOVE ME?

"If anyone loves me, he will obey my teaching."

John 14:23

DO I HAVE TO?

Do we love Jesus? Then we will do what He says. His way will not always be easy. And sometimes our friends will not like it at all. But God can see what we cannot. And He is working everything out for our good. . . .

You're **MAKING ME VERY ANGRY!**

G od's way is *always the best way*. So we should trust Him. And we should do what He says. One day our friends will see that Jesus is right. And we will laugh and enjoy His goodness *together!*

Lord, Teach Me to *Pray...*

L ord Jesus, I want to do things Your way. Please give me the courage to follow You. And help me to love my friends even when they are angry and do not understand.

DO YOU WANT TO?

The BEST of the STORY...

"If anyone loves me, he will obey my teaching. My Father will love him, and we will come to him and make our home with him."

John 14:23

The Final Word

Think About It!

*"Be still, and know that I am God."**

- Who (or what) holds the key to your heart?

- If **GOD** lives in your heart, has your life been honoring **HiM**?

- If God loved you when you **DiDN't** love Him, shouldn't you try to love and forgive your friend whether he deserves it or not?

I Believe
The Truth...

- I can LOVE.

- I can FORGIVE.

- I am listening. . . .

- I am GOD'S.

Psalm 46:10

Chapter Four

A True Believer

Jesus is alive right here in our hearts. . .

We have been born again!

Now our lives and everything in them belong to Him.

But where do we go from here?

We want to follow Jesus wherever He goes. But. . .

OH, HOW I LOVE JESUS!

Where

will that

LEAD US?

Let's Find out!

WHAT DOES GOD WANT?

"To obey is better than sacrifice."

1 Samuel 15:22

WHAT SHOULD I DO?

What does God want? Does He want us to give away all our money? Does He want us to live in a far-away place? Does He want us to stop watching TV? Should we try to stop eating so many snacks?

What does God want?!?

That's **a VERY GOOD QUESTION!**

And the answer is simple. . . . *God wants our hearts!* He wants us to be the living, breathing, absolutely real, visible expression of His one and only Son.

I CAN DO THAT!

Teach Me to Pray . . .

Lord Jesus, I want to know You. I want to be the person You long for me to be. Please help me to understand Your Word. And then help me to get up and do it.

God gives the best Gifts . . .

God wants to *give* me something. He wants to give me something real. . . . *He wants to give me Jesus!*

For God so loved the world that he gave his one and only Son, that whoever believes in him shall not perish but have eternal life.
John 3:16

BLAMING EVERYTHING ON THE DEVIL

And the Lord God commanded the man, "You are free to eat from any tree in the garden; but you must not eat from the tree of the knowledge of good and evil, for when you eat of it you will surely die."

Genesis 2:16–17

THE DEVIL MADE ME DO IT!

The devil is a liar. He wants us to hate and be angry. He wants us to do things that will break God's heart. *"Go ahead and sin,"* he will whisper. *"No one will ever find out. . . ."*

But **HERE'S the catch. . .**

The devil can try to make us do something wrong. *But it's up to us to do it.*

NO, YOU DID THAT ALL BY YOURSELF!

Lord, Teach Me to

Oh, Lord, please forgive me, for I have sinned. The devil laid a trap for me, and I walked right into it. I listened to his lie. I did just what he told me to do. Oh, Lord, I am so sorry. It's all my fault. Please forgive me. I want to be clean again.

The Sword of the

SPIRIT. . .

Which is the Word of God!

If we confess our sins, he is faithful and just and will forgive us our sins and purify us from all unrighteousness.
1 John 1:9

Resist the devil, and he will flee from you.
James 4:7

FeaR. . .NOT!

"Be strong
and courageous.
Do not be terrified...
for the Lord your God
will be with you
wherever you go."

Joshua 1:9

MY DAD IS BIG!

Are you afraid? God says *stop!* Jesus is here. And He is bigger and stronger than anything or anyone that will ever try to hurt you.

SO **Don't Even Think About It!**

Is something or someone trying to frighten us? Let's pray they don't get beat up too badly. Because for them to get to us, *they must get past Jesus first!*

YOU CAN SAY THAT AGAIN!

Lord, Teach Me to
Pray. . .

Thank You, Lord, for courage. Thank You for strength. I am not afraid. You are in control. Let the nations rage. You are God Almighty. And I am safe in the shelter of Your wings!

What the angel SAID. . .

"Do not be afraid. I bring you good news of great joy that will be for all the people. Today in the town of David a Savior has been born to you; he is Christ the Lord."

Luke 2:10–11

Give it Back!

For God hath not given us the spirit of fear; but of power, and of love, and of a sound mind.

2 Timothy 1:7 KJV

GET THAT THING AWAY FROM ME!

Are your knees knocking? Are your teeth chattering? Is your hair standing straight up on end? Someone is trying to give you the spirit of fear!

That's **No** BiG SURPRiSe

And that someone is the devil. But like everything that comes from the devil, *it is a big, fat lie!*

So Let's Take away the

Lie!

God will never leave us. He will never forsake us. He has loved us with an everlasting love. And at the name of Jesus, *every knee* in heaven and on earth must bow. And *every tongue* must confess that Jesus Christ is Lord to the glory of God the Father!

Everything is going to be alright.

I BELONG TO JESUS CHRIST!

The Word was.

THE WORD iS!

The Word will be. . .

Resist the devil, and he will flee from you.

James 4:7

He Will Flee From You!

Resist the devil, and he will flee from you.

James 4:7

GO BOTHER SOMEONE WHO'S LISTENING TO YOU...

The devil is a liar. There is no truth in him. He cannot stand to be in the presence of the light and power of Jesus Christ. So resist him! Hold up the cross so he can see it. Speak God's Word so that's all he can hear.

Get **RIGHT UP in His Face!**

Bring him to his knees: love! Crush him under your feet: forgive! Drive him back into the darkness: trust! Lock him up and throw away the keys: pray!

Lord, Teach Me to

Pray...

Thank You, Lord Jesus, for the cross! Thank You for washing my sins away! Thank You for Your awesome power. And thank You for allowing me to bear the mighty, Holy Name that is above all other Names. I love You.

I HAD NO IDEA HE COULD RUN SO FAST!

What does

Resist mean?

Resist: To refuse to accept, agree, or go along with someone or something.

TURNING AROUND

> *You intended to harm me, but God intended it for good to accomplish what is now being done, the saving of many lives.*
>
> *Genesis 50:20*

SATAN MEANT THIS FOR EVIL.

Bad things happen to good people. At times they seem to happen for no reason at all. We don't really understand it. And sometimes all we can say is "why?"

But God has not abandoned us. He did not forget or make a terrible mistake. . . .

It May Take Some Time

We may never know the reason why. But we can know this: God can see what we cannot. And even though it seems completely impossible right now, He is working all these "bad" things together *for our good.*

Teach Me to Pray...

Oh, Lord, I don't understand why this is happening. But I know that You are in control. And You will take this terrible pain and turn it into something beautiful.

BUT GOD TURNED IT INTO SOMETHING GOOD!

Something GOOD...

Be strong and take heart, all you who hope in the Lord.

Psalm 31:24

CHANGE

"I tell you the truth, unless you change and become like little children, you will never enter the kingdom of heaven."

Matthew 18:3

THIS COULD TAKE A WHILE!

Today you may be small. And you may be small again tomorrow. But you will not be small forever. . . .

Sometimes change happens quickly. And sometimes it can take a very long time.

You're **RiGHT ABØUt THat!**

*O*ur bodies may be little. But our souls are big. And something that big will take a long time to get right. . . .

And I Want It To Be

Right!

*B*ut God is not in a hurry. So we shouldn't be either.

He knows we're going to make a few mistakes. But that's okay. He will give us time to change. We can work to change with Him.

THAT'S OKAY. . . I CAN WAIT!

What to do with a
Mistake. . .

What do you do when you find a mistake?

You fix it, of course!

WHAT GOD IS. . .

God
is love.

1 John 4:8

I LOVE YOU.

Jesus loves us—mistakes
and all. We must always
remember this: God loves
us more than anyone
else can.

But **THaT Is a GOOD THING!**

Did someone hurt our feelings? That's terrible! Jesus would never do that!

But our friends are not Jesus.

You Can Say THAT

Again!

So we must never expect our friends to be perfect. For they are people just like us. Love is something people do every now and then. . . .

But love is what God is. And God is love all the time!

I LOVE YOU, TOO!

I was looking for

Love. . .

So I will not expect my friend to be perfect. She just can't do it. *And neither can I.*

But I can forgive her. And I can ask her to forgive me, too. Now we both can draw closer to Jesus—*together.*

BUT WHAT IS FAITH?

The just shall live by faith.

Hebrews 10:38 *KJV*

I CAN SEE THAT. . .

What is faith? It's really quite simple. Faith is being sure of what we hope for and certain of what we do not see!

And **THAT'S JUST HOW I LIVE**

So when things don't make sense, believe what *God* says. . . .

When we hear the word *can't*, say, "Oh yes *God can!*"

When all others are blind, let's see— *through God's eyes.*

And when all hope is gone, *watch Him come through!*

BUT CAN YOU DO IT?

YES, I DO!

God can do impossible things. . . .

Do I really believe this?

Then I will hold God's absolutely, *impossible* dream in my very own hands!

Faith, Please!

Without faith it is impossible to please God.

Hebrews 11:6

BUT WHY WOULD I FORGET TO TRUST HIM?

Do we want to please God? Then we must believe what He says. For God is not pleased when we refuse to trust Him. And who could blame Him? To not trust God is to call Him a liar. And we know that God is not a liar!

and **THAT IS THE TRUTH!**

But when we do trust Him, just the opposite is true! For God says that He will richly reward those who seek Him with all their heart.

Lord, Teach Me to
Pray...

Lord Jesus, please forgive me. I have forgotten how to trust You. And now my heart is empty. Please come and fill me again. I don't want to be tired and comfortable and safe. I want to be free and alive!

> EVERY WORD HE SAYS IS TRUE!

The rest of the
STORY...

Anyone who comes to him must believe that he exists and that he rewards those who earnestly seek him.

Hebrews 11:6

DoN'T HiDE. . .SEEK!

Seek the Lord
while he may
be found.

Isaiah 55:6

CANNONBALL!!!

Where is Jesus? What is He doing? Do we know? Do we care? We can float in happy circles on the sleepy surface of our lives. And that's fine. For God will bless us. But it will only be the blessing of having the tiniest part of one little toe dipped into the water. . . .

So WHaT'S WRONG WiTH one Toe?

But to get God's *reward*, we must jump in all the way. Yes, we may sink! Yes, we could drown! But we will sink into the embrace of His tender, mighty arms. And we will drown in the bottomless depths of His everlasting love!

Lord, Teach Me to
Pray...

*P*our out Your Spirit, Lord Jesus. Pour it out upon this sleepy little house. Flood me. Fill me. Drown me in Your amazing, wonderful love.

NOW *THAT WAS* A SPLASH!

Thus says the
LORD...

You will go out in joy and be led forth in peace; the mountains and hills will burst forth into song before you, and all the trees of the field will clap their hands.

Isaiah 55:12

Rise and Shine!

"No one lights a lamp and puts it in a place where it will be hidden. . . . Instead he puts it on its stand, so that those who come in may see the light."

Luke 11:33

HEY! WHO TURNED OUT THE LIGHTS?

Jesus changed our lives. We were like candles without flames. But when Jesus came into our hearts, what once was lifeless and cold suddenly became alive.

Then **It's Time to Dance!**

So let's not hide the new lives Jesus gave us. Let's live out in the open. Right where everyone can see. Our little light can chase the deepest darkness away.

But we must let it shine!

Lord, Teach Me to **Pray. . .**

Thank You, Jesus, *for all the good things You've done for me. Please open up the door to let me share them with my friends.*

IT'S NOT THE LIGHT. . . YOUR BATTERIES ARE DEAD!

Like a candle without a

Flame. . .

You can fill a dark room with hundreds of beautiful candles. But unless at least one of those candles is lit, everyone and everything will remain in the darkness.

A LoVe LiKe GoD'S

"Spread the corner of your garment over me, since you are a kinsman-redeemer."

Ruth 3:9

I WANT TO
BE LIKE YOU!

We can go to church. We can read our Bibles. We can worship and pray and spend time alone with Jesus. But to really be *like Him,* we must allow Him to change us. . . .

We must learn how to love.

But **WHAT'S SO HARD ABOUT THAT?**

> I WANT TO LEARN HOW TO LOVE. . .

I hated Jesus.
And He loved me.

I turned my back on
Him. And He loved me.

I used Him and abused
Him and cursed Him
beat Him and spat
right in His face!

So He spread
out His arms. . .

And as I nailed Him to
the cross, He whispered,
"I forgive you. . . ."

What's that mean for us?

Love. . .

And now we must
learn how to
do the same thing.

SUCCESS!

OOH BOY. . .I MAY ALREADY
BE A WINNER!

What is "success"?
Is it being famous? Having
a lot of money? That's what
everyone seems to think.
But listen to this: God
promised to give us the
desires of our hearts. He
promised to supply all our
needs. *We don't need to chase
after what we already have!*

So the real question is. . .

Are **OUR PLANS GOD'S PLANS?**

If they are, our plans are in good hands! For God's promise is to protect us and keep us safe for as long as it takes to work things out for our good according to His will.

Lord, Teach Me to

Pray...

Jesus, *You know my heart. I don't ever need to hide anything from You. Here are my plans, Lord. Teach me to hold on to what is good and let go of anything You desire to blow away.*

> ## I THOUGHT THIS WAS GOING TO BE EASY!!!

This is

Success

How does God define Success?

Am I trying to do what God wants me to do? Am I trying my best to do it in a way that pleases Him? *That is success!*

WEIGHT

> Lay aside every weight, and the sin which does so easily beset us, and let us run with patience the race that is set before us...
>
> Hebrews 12:1

PANT, GASP, WHEEZE!

Jesus asked us to follow Him. But sometimes He seems so far away. What went wrong?

We know we shouldn't be angry. And we know we need to forgive our friends. But the memory of all that has happened can seem to be sitting on our backs like a sack of wet sand. Is Jesus mad at us? No. But He does want us to unload all that stuff. He wants us to forgive our friends. *So let's forgive them.*

What **was I THINKING?**

*C*an we truly be God's and live each and every day of our lives pressed down and bent out of shape by the weight of anger, unforgiveness, jealousy, and hatred? Of course we can! *But why in the world would we want to?!?*

Lord, Teach Me to *Pray...*

Jesus, please show me the things in my life that keep me from walking freely with You. And give me the courage to lay them down and walk away.

> **DOES THIS MEAN I CAN'T HAVE A DONUT?**

What is **WEIGHT?**

How does God define Weight?

What is a weight? It's a heavy object used to hold something down (of course!). Satan will try to dump things like anger, jealousy, and unforgiveness into our hearts and minds. And then he'll work hard to keep them there. Why would he do that? It's simple. The thing Satan wants to weigh down *is us!*

THiS iS GOD'S WiLL!

Give thanks in all circumstances, for this is God's will for you in Christ Jesus.

1 Thessalonians 5:18

I Can Do This:

THANK YOU, JESUS!

It's easy to give thanks when things are going well. And things are going well! For God has given us so many blessings we don't have room enough to hold them. Did you remember to thank Him? That's good. . . .

But **can I DO THiS?**

Jesus says give thanks when things go wrong! Why? Because trouble will come! Are you happy? Give thanks! Is everything crashing down around you? God knows all about it! Jesus is here. His help will come. So give thanks!

Lord, Teach Me to *Pray...*

Lord, I don't understand why things turned out this way. But I know You are taking care of me. So I won't worry. I will trust You. And while I am waiting, I will give thanks.

THANK YOU, JESUS!

DANGER
SKUNKS &
POISON
IVY

And I **Quote...**

"In this world you will have trouble. But take heart! For I have overcome the world."

Jesus Christ, John 16:33

I can Do...

I can do everything through him who gives me strength.

Philippians 4:13

ALL THINGS!

ALL THINGS MEANS ALL THINGS...

I can do all things through Christ who gives me the strength. Do we really believe this? And what would we dare to do if we did?

Are **YOU TALKING TO ME?**

What are your dreams? Who do you want to become? Is it what God wants for you? Then you *can* do it. *And God will provide!*

Lord, Teach Me to **Pray...**

Jesus, *You know the one thing I want more than anything else in the world. My dreams belong to You. Please shape them with Your hands. Give me the courage to take You at Your word. And then give me the strength and faith to go out and do it.*

...OR IT DOESN'T MEAN ANYTHING!

How can I be **STRONG?**

Am I weak? *Then I am strong!* That's right! Jesus said, "My power is made perfect in weakness." Am I wimpy and wilted? Am I puny and small? *Perfect!* For when I trust in *God's word* and *God's power*, I become strong with *God's strength.*

Amen!

MORE

> *"Watch out! Be on guard against all kinds of greed; a man's life does not consist in the abundance of his possessions."*
>
> *Luke 12:15*

IS THIS ALL FOR ME?

How much do we need? Just a little bit more than we have, of course! But do we really need so many bigger, or better, or newer things? Sometimes the answer is *yes*. And God does promise to provide all our needs. . . . But He never said anything about providing all of our greeds.

No, **I GUESS HE DIDN'T!**

Do we have enough for today? Let's thank God. Do we have a little bit left over? Let's use it to help our friends!

Lord, Teach Me to

Pray...

Lord, You've given me everything I've ever wanted. Now please give me the grace to see beyond my own needs. Teach me to open my hands and my heart to help meet the needs of those around me.

KEEP IT COMING!

So how much is

EnOUGH...

And how in the world do I get It?

Jesus said, "Don't worry at all about having enough food and clothing (etc!). . . . Your heavenly Father already knows perfectly well that you need them, and He will give them to you if you give Him first place in your life and live as He wants you to."

See *Matthew 6:31–33*

223

MY Sin

> *If we confess our sins, he is faithful and just to forgive us our sins and purify us from all unrighteousness.*
>
> *1 John 1:9*

HOW CAN YOU EVER FORGIVE ME NOW?

The Bible says *all have sinned* and fall short of the glory of God.* So there's no need to kid ourselves. We know we have sinned. God knows, too. But what do we do now?

*Romans 3:23

Let's **Talk aBout Sin**

Jesus loves us—mistakes and all. But He hates our sin. And sin must be punished. For sin can destroy us—and will! But God is not about to let that happen. So Jesus said, "Father, punish Me instead." And He went to the cross and took the punishment we deserved for our sin.

DO WE HAVE TO ?!?

Lord, Teach Me to **Pray...**

Oh, Lord, You know what I've done. And I know, too. Please make me clean again by the power of the cleansing blood of Your Son Jesus Christ.

What does **Forgiveness** mean?

Jesus took my sin and nailed it to the cross. *He has removed our sins as far away from us as the east is from the west.** It is gone. Long gone!

And I can start over again, just as if I had never sinned.

*Psalm 103:12

PRaY!

> *My house will be called a house of prayer.*
>
> *Isaiah 56:7*

Is this God's house?

Where does God live? Where do we go to find Him? Is He in the church? The Bible says *wherever two or three come together in my name, there I am with them.** So yes, God is in the church, and the church is God's house. But what does God want His house to do? Well, for one thing, He wants His house to pray!

THIS IS GOD'S HOUSE.

*Matthew 18:20

Or **IS THIS GOD'S HOUSE?**

Now listen to this: *Your body is a temple of the Holy Spirit.** That's right! We are God's house, too! For God's Holy Spirit will come and live right here inside of our hearts. How can He do that? Just ask Him, and you'll see!

1 Corinthians 6:19

Lord, Teach Me to
Pray. . .

Lord Jesus, here is my heart. Please make my heart Your home. Sweep me clean of everything that makes You sad. And make this house Your house of prayer.

THIS IS GOD'S HOUSE!

Jesus loves the
CHURCH. . .

What is the Church?

The Church is everyone, everywhere who confesses that Jesus Christ is the one and only Son of the Living God who died on the cross and rose again to take our sins away.

New Clothes

Clothe yourselves with compassion, kindness, humility, gentleness and patience.

Colossians 3:12

THESE BABIES ARE GETTING TIGHT!

Anger. . . Hatred. . . Cursing. . . Lies. . .

Our old clothes just don't fit! We're not the same as we used to be. And we don't want to wear those old things anymore.

It's **TIME FOR SOMETHING NEW!**

Those clothes were just plain ugly. And they made us feel terrible, too. But now those things are gone! And everything is beautiful and new again.

Lord, Teach Me to
Pray. . .

Thank You, Lord Jesus, *for taking the old me and making me brand-new.*

I don't ever want to look or feel like I used to!

> AND THEY SMELL KIND OF FUNNY, TOO!

And I
Quote. . .

But now you must rid yourselves of all such things as these: anger, rage, malice, slander, and filthy language.

Colossians 3:8

THE FIRST STEP. . .

Clothe yourselves with compassion.

Colossians 3:12

I NEED SOME HELP DOWN HERE!!!

Before we knew Jesus, all we cared about was *ourselves*. We did things our own way. But our old selves do not fit anymore. Jesus does not look like that. And now neither can we.

Now **THAT'S WHAT I NEED!**

So let's set aside our feelings. Let's stop worrying about our needs. We've had enough of trying to make people listen to us. Let's stop and listen to them instead.

BUT WHAT ABOUT ME?

Lord, Teach Me to *Pray...*

Oh, Lord, I've made so many mistakes. I have hurt so many people. Please teach me how to love the way You do. I want to be like You.

How can I be **Compassionate?**

Is my friend angry? Hurting? Obnoxious? Wrong? I will not judge. I will not blame. I will not turn and walk away. I will listen. I will care. And if he will let me. . .*I will help.*

IT'S THAT SIMPLE!

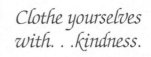

Clothe yourselves with. . .kindness.

Colossians 3:12

THIS IS FOR YOU!

Kindness is a simple thing. It is done best by simple hands. It is heard best in simple words. It is seen most clearly in simple gifts. It beats the loudest in a simple heart.

But **That Seems So Simple!**

Is your friend hungry? Feed him. Is he thirsty? Give him a drink. Has your friend become your enemy? Forgive him *and love him just the same.*

YOU ARE MY FRIEND.

Lord, Teach Me to

Pray...

Oh, Lord, I am so busy. Please make me simple and quiet again.

Simply Beautiful...

What can I do to help someone today? Before this beautiful day has slipped away, *I will do it.*

MR. BiG

> *Clothe yourselves with. . .humility.*
>
> *Colossians 3:12*

I AM THE RULER OF THE WORLD!

$\overset{\circ}{A}$re we big and bold and loud and proud, elaborate, extreme, pretentious and showy?

Well. . .

You're **BLOCKING the view!**

If everyone is looking at us and our amazing, glittering, glorious selves. . .how will they ever be able to see Jesus?

Lord, Teach Me to
Pray. . .

Forgive me for standing in front of You, Jesus. You are God. And I am not.

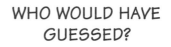

WHO WOULD HAVE GUESSED?

And I Quote. . .

God opposes the proud but gives grace to the humble.

James 4:6

BUTTERFLY OR STEAMROLLER?

Clothe yourselves with. . .gentleness.

Colossians 3:12

LOOK. . .A BUTTERFLY!

Are you a butterfly or a steamroller? It isn't hard to tell. Do you shine with the gentle light of God's love? Or do you use what you know about God to hurt other people's feelings?

Are **WE HAVING ANY FUN YET?**

It's easy to stomp all over people with our beliefs and opinions. And sometimes it's fun, too! But Jesus says *stop*. That is not God's way. And it must not be our way either.

THANK YOU, JESUS

Lord, Teach Me to *Pray...*

Lord Jesus, please forgive me for stomping all over my friends. Your love is a gift, not a weapon. And I want to share it with Your gentle, loving hands.

No **PRESSURE...**

Gentle or Severe?

Gentle: *Using little pressure so that the effects are not severe.*

Severe: *Causing great pain by being extreme.*

THE BIG ONE!

Clothe yourselves with. . .patience.

Colossians 3:12

ANYTHING BUT THAT!

We can wait. . .*at least for a little while!* And that's good. Just about anyone can learn how to wait!

But Jesus did not ask us to clothe ourselves with *waiting*. He asked us to clothe ourselves with *patience*. So what's the difference?

Now, **wait JUST one Minute!**

To wait is to stop in one place and do nothing until something happens. And that's easy enough. . . .

Okay. . .I'm

Waiting!

But when we can *wait* without becoming anxious or upset. . .when we can *do nothing* while our friends all move on. . . when we can *stay in one place* without complaining, no matter how hard it gets. . .

That is patience!

THIS COULD TAKE A WHILE. . .

Come on, let's

Go. . .

Imitate those who through faith and patience inherit what has been promised.

Hebrews 6:12

GRIN AND BEAR IT!

Bear with each other.

Colossians 3:13

I AM WHAT I AM!

*O*ur friends are not perfect. And we would like to fix them. But that would just make things worse. . . . They would all be just as imperfect as we are!

Now **THAT'S WHAT I want!**

Do we want friends who will fix us? Or do we want friends who will love us for who we are?

Do we want a friend who will point out everything we do wrong? Or do we want one who will help us to stand when we're about to fall down?

I KNOW WHAT YOU'RE THINKING, BUT I'M NOT GOING TO SAY IT!

Lord, Teach Me to **Pray...**

Lord Jesus, I want to be a true friend. Please help me to see what You see. I want to love and forgive the way that You do.

The rest of the **STORY...**

Bear with each other and forgive whatever grievances you may have against one another. Forgive as the Lord forgave you.

Colossians 3:13

ROCK MUSIC!

The whole crowd of disciples began joyfully to praise God in loud voices for all the miracles they had seen.

Luke 19:37

WHOAH, DUDE! THESE ROCKS CAN ROCK!

Has God been good to you? Then you should thank Him! For if you don't, Jesus says the *rocks* will rise up and begin to sing His praise!

Thing, **THING. THAT THING Can Sing!**

So go ahead and praise Him for all the amazing things He has done! God is good! And if someone is going to rock. . . *He wants it to be you!*

> DUDE, THOSE ROCKS CAN ROCK AROUND THE CLOCK!

Lord, Teach Me to Pray. . .

Thank You, Lord Jesus, for all of the beautiful things You have brought into my life. You are God Almighty. And You are worthy of my praise. Hallelujah!

The rest of the STORY. . .

Some of the Pharisees in the crowd said to Jesus, "Teacher, rebuke your disciples!"

"I tell you," he replied, "if they keep quiet, the stones will cry out."

Luke 19:39–40

HUNGRY LIONS

My God sent his angel, and he shut the mouths of the lions. They have not hurt me, because I was found innocent in his sight.

Daniel 6:22

NICE KITTY!

Are we alone? Are we in the dark? Have we been surrounded by hungry lions? God knows where we are. He did not leave us. He is right here beside us.

A Really Big Show

The people who set this trap for us are watching. They think they hurt us. But they are about to get a big surprise!

CAT GOT YOUR TONGUE?

Can I Get an Amen?

For God can do impossible things. So we will trust Him. And we will see with our eyes and hear with our ears and touch and taste and know *for real* that God is good. He will deliver us from our enemies. Amen!

The rest of the STORY. . .

And when Daniel was lifted from the den, no wound was found on him, because he had trusted in his God.

Daniel 6:23

THe Same OLD THiNG!

There is
nothing new
under the sun.

Ecclesiastes 1:9

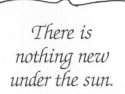

HERE WE GO AGAIN...

This day is pretty much the same as any other day. . . .

We will rise to the music of a thousand birds singing. The gentle morning sun will cause these sleepy flowers to lift their heads once again.

I've **seen it all before**

We will run the same grassy path, splash the same sparkling water, and climb a mile high into the shade of the same twisted, green tree.

When the Sun **begins to set...**

We will gather at the same table, with the same people, to say the same prayer. . . .

THANK YOU, JESUS!

Good night Moon. . .

And as we crawl into bed and stare up into the endless, starry sky, we will close our eyes and whisper the very same thing we do every night. . .

Thank You, Jesus. Thank You for the same old thing.

BECOMING

"Do you think that in such a short time you can persuade me to be a Christian?"

Acts 26:28

I BELIEVE JESUS!

Yes, we can tell people about Jesus, and sometimes it never seems to make a difference. . . .

Where **DiD ALL MY FRiENDS GO?**

Paul went to *prison* for telling people about Jesus. But did he let that stop him? No! *He wrote the Bible there!*

Until
Next
TIME. . .

So we can't give up either.

Let's love our friends and stop trying to fix them. Let's give our lives to Jesus and let Him *fix us* instead. Jesus can change the hardest heart. And we ought to know. . .

Because He changed *you* just like He changed *me!*

AND NOW I DO, TOO!

Yes, Lord,
I BELiEVE. . .

Paul replied, "Short time or long—I pray God that not only you but all who are listening to me today may become what I am, except for these chains."

Acts 26:29

"I am the resurrection and the life. He who believes in me will live, even though he dies; and whoever lives and believes in me will never die. Do you believe this?"

Index...

Index...